The *Reflective Bible Journal for Teens* led m
reading and understanding more about the
Word using the five R's. The journal is filled with suggestions for teens on how
you can make Bible reflection a daily process. I liked that it included resources
such as a Scripture reading plan, advice on how to restore relationships, and
memory verses. I recommend this for teens who want to ask questions about the
Bible and need a resource that will help them discover a love for reading God's
Word.

— ELIANA WARD, TEEN AND *BOXED POETRY* MAGAZINE EDITOR

The *Reflective Bible Journal* is an amazing way to guide your time with the Lord. I
used to be unsure of how to spend time with God. The *Reflective Bible Journal* is
an amazing guide that I continue to use.

— COURTNEY D., TEEN

The *Reflective Bible Journal* is an amazing resource to help you dive deeper into
devotions in a way you wouldn't normally engage with some Bible texts. It is full
of rich insight and overall a positive commitment.

— JENN N., TEEN

The *Reflective Bible Journal* gives a space for teens to learn how to listen to God's
voice and reflect on his Word. I looked forward to it each and every morning.
Taryn's words brought me closer to God and made me really want to dive deeper
and study Scripture more in depth than I ever have. I loved every second of
reflective journaling I had, and if you are looking for a way to get into God's Word
and reflect on it, this is it.

— LILY H., TEEN

This journal is very helpful to me because I feel like it is bringing me closer to
God. I get to read his word and think on it. I can already see where it is helping
me go in my life.

— ALICIA P., TEEN

I had the honor of piloting the *Reflective Bible Journal for Teens* with a high school student that I mentor. The journal completely lit up her heart! She even took it on vacation with her and did the study with a friend on their trip. Picture two high school girls sitting around the campfire, reading a passage of the Bible together, and then writing their reflections in the journal. You know when a journal lights up the hearts of high school students like that, it is really special! The world is about to be changed for the better as teens learn to engage and reflect on their Bible reading in ways that really connect with them.

— KELLIE LA FOLLETTE, WRITER & MENTOR

I love that this journal gives my teenager something to help her stay connected to God and reflect on things that are going on in her life, both good and bad. As a parent, I appreciate that this journal helps my teenager stay centered in God and reminds her she can look to God's word for guidance and answers to her questions. It warms my heart to know that she is spending quality time with God almost every day of the week. This journal has been an answer to my prayers.

— LISA PATTERSON, PARENT

Reflective Bible Journal

FOR TEENS

TARYN NERGAARD

typewriter creative co.

typewriter
creative co.

www.tarynnergaard.com

Edited by Jennie G. Scott.

Cover & interior design by Typewriter Creative Co. Cover graphics by Basia Stryjecka on CreativeMarket.com.

ISBN 978-1-7770331-3-2 (Paperback)

you are loved

contents

hey there...

I'm Taryn. At the time of publishing this journal, I'm a 33-year-old mom of four. I graduated from high school 15 years ago. What I'm trying to get at is my teen years were a long time ago.

I can't relate to what it's like to be a teenager in the 2020's and beyond. You're dealing with things I never had to deal with. But regardless of what decade we're in as teenagers, the hope of Jesus is always relevant.

This journal that I created for you is what I wish I had when I was your age. I didn't know how to hear God's voice, and I certainly wasn't following his plan for my life.

But you can. And this journal will help you.

On the following pages you'll find my recommendations for using this journal. Before you read it, I want you to know that your life with God is never about perfection. It's about progress. Spending time with God isn't about earning his love; we already have that in abundance!

Treat your time with God like the time you spend with a friend get to know him, talk to him, listen to him, hang out with him.

Come as you are. *God simply wants to spend time with you.*

using the journal

On the following pages you'll find recommendations for how to use this journal. I want to help you make the most out of this journal, but I call these recommendations rather than instructions because I trust that God will lead you through your daily time with him.

In addition to this *Using the Journal* section, be sure to flip to the back of the book to the *Resources* section as I've provided additional content for you.

Daily Bible Reading

Studying your Bible is important. It's good to know the meaning behind specific words and to understand the culture of when the Bible was written. Great insights can be learned by doing a Bible study.

But sometimes, in our quest to learn more about the Bible, we forget to apply the truths of the Bible to our current lives.

This journal will help you use your daily Bible reading time to connect with God in a new way. It will guide you into an active conversation with God that will deepend your relationship with him and help you apply what God teaches you through your reading and reflection.

When we strengthen our conversation skills with God through the Bible, we gain a better understanding of our purpose, our direction, and our immediate next steps. This wisdom equips us to glorify God and build his Kingdom here on earth.

What You Need

To read God's word, you need a Bible. For this method, I recommend a physical Bible, but the YouVersion Bible app is a good second choice. Choose a translation of the Bible you can easily understand. The Christian Standard Bible is my current favorite. Additionally, have this journal and a pen or pencil ready.

What to Read

Pick a book of the Bible and read 5-15 verses each day. For this method of Bible reading, it's best to read a smaller passage that you can remember and apply to your life rather than a large passage that overwhelms you with too much information.

After you finish your reflection time using this journal, you can go back to your Bible and read more if you'd like.

Tip: If you're new to reading the Bible, start in the New Testament. Or, try the reading plan in the resource section.

Write it Down

When we want to remember something important, we write it down. We should do the same thing when we spend time with God. Expect him to speak to you!

On your daily journal pages, write the date and reflect on how you are feeling at the moment. Be as specific as possible. It's okay if you need to sit still and silent for a few minutes to recognize what's going on inside your heart. If recognizing your emotions is difficult or new for you, see the *Resources* section for help.

Next, follow the format as you go through the steps.

- Read
- Receive (no journal space for this prompt)
- Reflect
- Respond
- Remember

READ

Start reading. When something stands out to you, use your pen to place a mark in your Bible. Marking with a pen or pencil gives you more options than simply highlighting everything.

I use a small tick (`) to note something that stood out to me. For parts that really catch my attention, I use square brackets ([ ]) around the phrase. For single words that seem significant or are repeated, I use an underline (_).

Choose what works best for you. The purpose is to notice when something stands out to you or when you make a connection with something else you've read.

In your journal, write down the verses you read. You can also include a summary of what stood out to you in your own words.

For example:

James 1:19-21 - Be quick to listen and slow to speak...

RECEIVE

After you've written down the part of the passage that stood out to you, pray. Ask God what he wants you to know after reading those verses.

Dig deeper by asking specific questions:

- What do you want to teach me with this verse?
- How does this verse apply to my day today?
- Is there something you would like me to start doing?
- Is there something you would like me to stop doing?

Through this process, you are engaging in conversation with God regarding what he wants to talk to you about or teach you.

REFLECT

Now take time to write down what you feel God spoke to you. It's okay if you're not sure. Write it down anyway. If you don't think you heard anything, try closing your eyes again and listen. Or, write down what you already know about God. For example: God loves me.

Next, write down one thing you can trust God with today. Think of any situations that are causing you to feel anxious or confused, or even something coming up that you're excited about.

No matter how big or how little, anything going on inside of us or in our lives is something we can give to God and trust him to take care of for us.

RESPOND

Now is the time to continue the conversation with God through prayer. Thank God for his faithfulness in your life, the truths he is teaching you, or anything else for which you feel grateful.

It's at this point in my own routine that I bring my wants, needs, and desires to God. By focusing on learning from him first and then bringing my needs to him second, I come before him with a humble, open heart.

Write your prayers in your journal as a way to recall past requests and remind yourself of his faithfulness.

REMEMBER

Write out a verse to memorize this week. Writing it out will help you to remember it, and being able to recall Scripture is an important part of connecting your daily life to God's presence.

If you find Scripture memorization challenging, don't put pressure on yourself to memorize a new verse each week. Simply repeat the same verse until you're ready to move on.

A Note About the Holy Spirit

When Jesus went to heaven, he promised the disciples that he would send them a helper. He kept his promise and sent the Holy Spirit to be with the disciples. Anyone who loves God and follows Jesus also has the Holy Spirit as a helper. The Spirit comforts us, guides us, and speaks to us.

The way the Holy Spirit speaks to us is different than the way we hear from our parents, siblings, and friends. The Spirit speaks more like a kind thought in your mind or a warm feeling in your body.

Every day is a new day to practice listening for God's voice. If you're not sure about what God is speaking to you, that's normal. But God is glad you're taking the time to listen, regardless of your uncertainty.

Weekly Reflection

The *Weekly Reflection* is an opportunity to recognize what is going well and where you're facing disappointment or anxiety. Paying attention to our lives is an important skill for our emotional, physical, and spiritual growth.

PERSONAL REFLECTION

Be honest and allow yourself to celebrate the highs and make space for the lows. We cannot grow from a place of shame, so it's best to "make friends" with all the parts of ourselves, even the uncomfortable parts.

By ending with gratitude, we teach ourselves that we can have thankful hearts regardless of what's going on in our lives.

RELATIONAL REFLECTION

It's important to pay attention to our relationships. Between family, friends, teachers, and coaches, there may be times in our week when conflicts arise. Or, sometimes we struggle with our own emotions and let them affect the people around us. This section is an opportunity to recognize what's going well in our relationships and what could be better in our relationships. Awareness is always the first step in our growth.

SPIRITUAL REFLECTION

This section of your *Weekly Reflection* helps pull together your daily time with God. Look back through your *Reflect* writing from each day and identify any similar messages you felt God speak to you.

Has God been affirming similar ideas or truths to you through other sources? This is the place to make those connections and recognize all the ways God is speaking to you regularly.

After your week of spending daily time with God, are there any questions you have for him? Don't be afraid to search your heart and mind for areas of doubt you are facing. God can handle our questions and doubts—it does not mean we lack faith!

Remember, you are already loved and God enjoys spending time with you.

NEXT WEEK

It's important to have something to look forward to. It can be anything of any size—as long as it brings you joy! If you can't think of anything you are looking forward to, plan something now.

Is there something you're worried about when you think of next week? Write it down and consider who you can talk to about it or ask for help. Most importantly, take a moment to pray.

Resources

In the back of the journal, you'll find additional resources to support your personal, relational, and spiritual growth. All of these are optional, so use only what you find helpful.

- memory verses
- list of emotions
- reading plan
- help for restoring relationships
- prayer of forgiveness
- prayer of repentance
- prayer for an anxious heart

You can see a sample of the journal on the following pages. Some days you'll fill the whole space, other times you might only write a few words.

date: January 1, 2020

Today, I feel: isolated & disappointed

READ

Today, I read: Philippians 1:1-14

What stood out to me is:

Verse 6... "he who began a good work in you will carry it out to completion..."

REFLECT

What I best sense God speaking to me is:

He is faithful. I don't need to know all the answers or see what's coming in the future--I can trust that God is working out the details. Have faith!

One thing I will trust God with today is:

Whether or not I get the job.

RESPOND

God, thank you for reminding me not to worry because you are in control. Help me to trust you when I'm feeling overwhelmed and anxious. Please show what is important to focus on today and help me let go of everything else. Be with me today as I parent and work--give me patience and love for everyone I'm around today. Thank you God. Amen.

REMEMBER

Romans 8:5-6

For those who live according to the flesh have their minds set on the things of the flesh, but those who live according to the Spirit have their minds set on the things of the Spirit. Now the mind-set of the flesh is death, but the mind-set of the Spirit is life and peace.

weekly reflection: Dec 30 - Jan 5, 2020

PERSONAL REFLECTION

What went well this week?

> We had a relaxing time over the holidays as a family. I didn't get anxious about things that weren't important.

What feeling(s) did I experience most frequently? Why?

> Isolated, lonely. The holidays remind me that people around me don't know me very well. It would be nice to feel truly seen and known.

Three things I am grateful for are:

1. My family

2. Holiday celebrations

3. Church

RELATIONAL REFLECTION

What went well in my relationships this week?

> I spent yesterday with my brother and we got along well.

What felt challenging in my relationships this week?

> I lost my patience with Becca. Jessica didn't call me when she said she would.

SPIRITUAL REFLECTION

A theme God has been speaking to me this week through Bible reading, worship, books, or sermons:

> That everyone feels rejection. I should still choose to connect with people and not feel hurt when relationships don't feel equal.

Questions I have for God are:

> Why are friendships so hard??

NEXT WEEK

I am looking forward to...

> Going to the mall with Becca and going to the cabin with my family.

Next week's memory verse:

> Romans 8:37-39

journal

date:

Today, I feel:

READ

Today, I read:

What stood out to me is:

REFLECT

What I best sense God speaking to me is:

One thing I will trust God with today is:

RESPOND

REMEMBER

date:

Today, I feel:

READ

Today, I read:

What stood out to me is:

REFLECT

What I best sense God speaking to me is:

One thing I will trust God with today is:

RESPOND

REMEMBER

date:

Today, I feel:

READ

Today, I read:

What stood out to me is:

REFLECT

What I best sense God speaking to me is:

One thing I will trust God with today is:

RESPOND

REMEMBER

date:

Today, I feel:

READ

Today, I read:

What stood out to me is:

REFLECT

What I best sense God speaking to me is:

One thing I will trust God with today is:

RESPOND

REMEMBER

date: ....

Today, I feel: ....

READ

Today, I read: ....

What stood out to me is:

REFLECT

What I best sense God speaking to me is:

One thing I will trust God with today is:

RESPOND

REMEMBER

weekly reflection: ....

PERSONAL REFLECTION

What went well this week?

What feeling(s) did I experience most frequently? Why?

Three things I am grateful for are:

1.

2.

3.

RELATIONAL REFLECTION

What went well in my relationships this week?

What felt challenging in my relationships this week?

A theme God has been speaking to me this week through Bible reading, worship, books, or sermons:

Questions I have for God are:

NEXT WEEK

I am looking forward to...

Next week's memory verse:

33

date: ....

Today, I feel: ....

READ

Today, I read: ....

What stood out to me is:

::

REFLECT

What I best sense God speaking to me is:

::

One thing I will trust God with today is:

::

RESPOND

REMEMBER

date:

Today, I feel:

READ

Today, I read:

What stood out to me is:

REFLECT

What I best sense God speaking to me is:

One thing I will trust God with today is:

RESPOND

REMEMBER

date:

Today, I feel:

READ

Today, I read:

What stood out to me is:

REFLECT

What I best sense God speaking to me is:

One thing I will trust God with today is:

RESPOND

REMEMBER

date:

Today, I feel:

READ

Today, I read:

What stood out to me is:

REFLECT

What I best sense God speaking to me is:

One thing I will trust God with today is:

RESPOND

REMEMBER

date:

Today, I feel:

READ

Today, I read:

What stood out to me is:

REFLECT

What I best sense God speaking to me is:

One thing I will trust God with today is:

RESPOND

REMEMBER

weekly reflection: ....

PERSONAL REFLECTION

What went well this week?

What feeling(s) did I experience most frequently? Why?

Three things I am grateful for are:

1.

2.

3.

RELATIONAL REFLECTION

What went well in my relationships this week?

What felt challenging in my relationships this week?

SPIRITUAL REFLECTION

A theme God has been speaking to me this week through Bible reading, worship, books, or sermons:

Questions I have for God are:

NEXT WEEK

I am looking forward to...

Next week's memory verse:

date: ....

Today, I feel: ....

READ

Today, I read: ....

What stood out to me is:

REFLECT

What I best sense God speaking to me is:

One thing I will trust God with today is:

RESPOND

REMEMBER

date:

Today, I feel:

R E A D

Today, I read:

What stood out to me is:

R E F L E C T

What I best sense God speaking to me is:

One thing I will trust God with today is:

RESPOND

REMEMBER

date: ....

Today, I feel: ....

READ

Today, I read: ....

What stood out to me is:

> (blank box)

REFLECT

What I best sense God speaking to me is:

> (blank box)

One thing I will trust God with today is:

> (blank box)

RESPOND

REMEMBER

date:

Today, I feel:

READ

Today, I read:

What stood out to me is:

REFLECT

What I best sense God speaking to me is:

One thing I will trust God with today is:

RESPOND

REMEMBER

date: ....

Today, I feel: ....

READ

Today, I read: ....

What stood out to me is:

REFLECT

What I best sense God speaking to me is:

One thing I will trust God with today is:

RESPOND

REMEMBER

weekly reflection: ....

PERSONAL REFLECTION

What went well this week?

What feeling(s) did I experience most frequently? Why?

Three things I am grateful for are:

1.

2.

3.

RELATIONAL REFLECTION

What went well in my relationships this week?

What felt challenging in my relationships this week?

SPIRITUAL REFLECTION

A theme God has been speaking to me this week through Bible reading, worship, books, or sermons:

Questions I have for God are:

NEXT WEEK

I am looking forward to...

Next week's memory verse:

date:

Today, I feel:

READ

Today, I read:

What stood out to me is:

REFLECT

What I best sense God speaking to me is:

One thing I will trust God with today is:

RESPOND

REMEMBER

date:

Today, I feel:

READ

Today, I read:

What stood out to me is:

REFLECT

What I best sense God speaking to me is:

One thing I will trust God with today is:

RESPOND

REMEMBER

date: ....

Today, I feel: ....

READ

Today, I read: ....

What stood out to me is:

REFLECT

What I best sense God speaking to me is:

One thing I will trust God with today is:

RESPOND

REMEMBER

date:

Today, I feel:

READ

Today, I read:

What stood out to me is:

REFLECT

What I best sense God speaking to me is:

One thing I will trust God with today is:

RESPOND

REMEMBER

date:

Today, I feel:

READ

Today, I read:

What stood out to me is:

REFLECT

What I best sense God speaking to me is:

One thing I will trust God with today is:

RESPOND

REMEMBER

weekly reflection: ....

PERSONAL REFLECTION

What went well this week?

What feeling(s) did I experience most frequently? Why?

Three things I am grateful for are:

1.

2.

3.

RELATIONAL REFLECTION

What went well in my relationships this week?

What felt challenging in my relationships this week?

SPIRITUAL REFLECTION

A theme God has been speaking to me this week through Bible reading, worship, books, or sermons:

Questions I have for God are:

NEXT WEEK

I am looking forward to...

Next week's memory verse:

date: ....

Today, I feel: ....

READ

Today, I read: ....

What stood out to me is:

REFLECT

What I best sense God speaking to me is:

One thing I will trust God with today is:

RESPOND

REMEMBER

date:

Today, I feel:

READ

Today, I read:

What stood out to me is:

REFLECT

What I best sense God speaking to me is:

One thing I will trust God with today is:

RESPOND

REMEMBER

date: ....

Today, I feel: ....

READ

Today, I read: ....

What stood out to me is:

REFLECT

What I best sense God speaking to me is:

One thing I will trust God with today is:

RESPOND

REMEMBER

date: ....

Today, I feel: ....

READ

Today, I read: ....

What stood out to me is:

[ ]

REFLECT

What I best sense God speaking to me is:

[ ]

One thing I will trust God with today is:

[ ]

RESPOND

REMEMBER

date:

Today, I feel:

READ

Today, I read:

What stood out to me is:

REFLECT

What I best sense God speaking to me is:

One thing I will trust God with today is:

RESPOND

REMEMBER

weekly reflection: ....

PERSONAL REFLECTION

What went well this week?

[ ]

What feeling(s) did I experience most frequently? Why?

[ ]

Three things I am grateful for are:

1.

2.

3.

RELATIONAL REFLECTION

What went well in my relationships this week?

[ ]

What felt challenging in my relationships this week?

SPIRITUAL REFLECTION

A theme God has been speaking to me this week through Bible reading, worship, books, or sermons:

Questions I have for God are:

NEXT WEEK

I am looking forward to...

Next week's memory verse:

date:

Today, I feel:

READ

Today, I read:

What stood out to me is:

REFLECT

What I best sense God speaking to me is:

One thing I will trust God with today is:

RESPOND

REMEMBER

date:

Today, I feel:

READ

Today, I read:

What stood out to me is:

REFLECT

What I best sense God speaking to me is:

One thing I will trust God with today is:

RESPOND

REMEMBER

date:

Today, I feel:

READ

Today, I read:

What stood out to me is:

REFLECT

What I best sense God speaking to me is:

One thing I will trust God with today is:

RESPOND

REMEMBER

date:

Today, I feel:

READ

Today, I read:

What stood out to me is:

REFLECT

What I best sense God speaking to me is:

One thing I will trust God with today is:

RESPOND

REMEMBER

date:

Today, I feel:

READ

Today, I read:

What stood out to me is:

REFLECT

What I best sense God speaking to me is:

One thing I will trust God with today is:

RESPOND

REMEMBER

weekly reflection: ....

PERSONAL REFLECTION

What went well this week?

What feeling(s) did I experience most frequently? Why?

Three things I am grateful for are:

1.

2.

3.

RELATIONAL REFLECTION

What went well in my relationships this week?

What felt challenging in my relationships this week?

SPIRITUAL REFLECTION

A theme God has been speaking to me this week through Bible reading, worship, books, or sermons:

Questions I have for God are:

NEXT WEEK

I am looking forward to...

Next week's memory verse:

date:

Today, I feel:

READ

Today, I read:

What stood out to me is:

REFLECT

What I best sense God speaking to me is:

One thing I will trust God with today is:

RESPOND

REMEMBER

date:

Today, I feel:

READ

Today, I read:

What stood out to me is:

REFLECT

What I best sense God speaking to me is:

One thing I will trust God with today is:

RESPOND

REMEMBER

date:

Today, I feel:

READ

Today, I read:

What stood out to me is:

REFLECT

What I best sense God speaking to me is:

One thing I will trust God with today is:

RESPOND

REMEMBER

date: ....

Today, I feel: ....

R E A D

Today, I read: ....

What stood out to me is:

R E F L E C T

What I best sense God speaking to me is:

One thing I will trust God with today is:

RESPOND

REMEMBER

date:

Today, I feel:

READ

Today, I read:

What stood out to me is:

REFLECT

What I best sense God speaking to me is:

One thing I will trust God with today is:

RESPOND

REMEMBER

weekly reflection: ....

PERSONAL REFLECTION

What went well this week?

What feeling(s) did I experience most frequently? Why?

Three things I am grateful for are:

1.

2.

3.

RELATIONAL REFLECTION

What went well in my relationships this week?

What felt challenging in my relationships this week?

SPIRITUAL REFLECTION

A theme God has been speaking to me this week through Bible reading, worship, books, or sermons:

Questions I have for God are:

NEXT WEEK

I am looking forward to...

Next week's memory verse:

date:

Today, I feel:

READ

Today, I read:

What stood out to me is:

REFLECT

What I best sense God speaking to me is:

One thing I will trust God with today is:

RESPOND

REMEMBER

date:

Today, I feel:

READ

Today, I read:

What stood out to me is:

REFLECT

What I best sense God speaking to me is:

One thing I will trust God with today is:

RESPOND

REMEMBER

date:

Today, I feel:

READ

Today, I read:

What stood out to me is:

REFLECT

What I best sense God speaking to me is:

One thing I will trust God with today is:

RESPOND

REMEMBER

date:

Today, I feel:

READ

Today, I read:

What stood out to me is:

REFLECT

What I best sense God speaking to me is:

One thing I will trust God with today is:

RESPOND

REMEMBER

date:

Today, I feel:

READ

Today, I read:

What stood out to me is:

REFLECT

What I best sense God speaking to me is:

One thing I will trust God with today is:

RESPOND

REMEMBER

weekly reflection: ....

PERSONAL REFLECTION

What went well this week?

What feeling(s) did I experience most frequently? Why?

Three things I am grateful for are:

1.

2.

3.

RELATIONAL REFLECTION

What went well in my relationships this week?

What felt challenging in my relationships this week?

A theme God has been speaking to me this week through Bible reading, worship, books, or sermons:

Questions I have for God are:

NEXT WEEK

I am looking forward to...

Next week's memory verse:

date:

Today, I feel:

READ

Today, I read:

What stood out to me is:

REFLECT

What I best sense God speaking to me is:

One thing I will trust God with today is:

RESPOND

REMEMBER

date:

Today, I feel:

READ

Today, I read:

What stood out to me is:

REFLECT

What I best sense God speaking to me is:

One thing I will trust God with today is:

RESPOND

REMEMBER

date:

Today, I feel:

READ

Today, I read:

What stood out to me is:

REFLECT

What I best sense God speaking to me is:

One thing I will trust God with today is:

RESPOND

REMEMBER

date:

Today, I feel:

READ

Today, I read:

What stood out to me is:

REFLECT

What I best sense God speaking to me is:

One thing I will trust God with today is:

RESPOND

REMEMBER

date:

Today, I feel:

READ

Today, I read:

What stood out to me is:

REFLECT

What I best sense God speaking to me is:

One thing I will trust God with today is:

RESPOND

REMEMBER

weekly reflection: _____

PERSONAL REFLECTION

What went well this week?

What feeling(s) did I experience most frequently? Why?

Three things I am grateful for are:

1.

2.

3.

RELATIONAL REFLECTION

What went well in my relationships this week?

What felt challenging in my relationships this week?

SPIRITUAL REFLECTION

A theme God has been speaking to me this week through Bible reading, worship, books, or sermons:

Questions I have for God are:

NEXT WEEK

I am looking forward to...

Next week's memory verse:

date:

Today, I feel:

READ

Today, I read:

What stood out to me is:

REFLECT

What I best sense God speaking to me is:

One thing I will trust God with today is:

RESPOND

REMEMBER

date:

Today, I feel:

READ

Today, I read:

What stood out to me is:

REFLECT

What I best sense God speaking to me is:

One thing I will trust God with today is:

RESPOND

REMEMBER

date:

Today, I feel:

READ

Today, I read:

What stood out to me is:

REFLECT

What I best sense God speaking to me is:

One thing I will trust God with today is:

RESPOND

REMEMBER

date:

Today, I feel:

READ

Today, I read:

What stood out to me is:

REFLECT

What I best sense God speaking to me is:

One thing I will trust God with today is:

RESPOND

REMEMBER

date:

Today, I feel:

READ

Today, I read:

What stood out to me is:

REFLECT

What I best sense God speaking to me is:

One thing I will trust God with today is:

RESPOND

REMEMBER

weekly reflection: ....

PERSONAL REFLECTION

What went well this week?

What feeling(s) did I experience most frequently? Why?

Three things I am grateful for are:

1.

2.

3.

RELATIONAL REFLECTION

What went well in my relationships this week?

What felt challenging in my relationships this week?

A theme God has been speaking to me this week through Bible reading, worship, books, or sermons:

Questions I have for God are:

NEXT WEEK

I am looking forward to...

Next week's memory verse:

date:

Today, I feel:

R E A D

Today, I read:

What stood out to me is:

R E F L E C T

What I best sense God speaking to me is:

One thing I will trust God with today is:

RESPOND

REMEMBER

date:

Today, I feel:

READ

Today, I read:

What stood out to me is:

REFLECT

What I best sense God speaking to me is:

One thing I will trust God with today is:

RESPOND

REMEMBER

date:

Today, I feel:

READ

Today, I read:

What stood out to me is:

REFLECT

What I best sense God speaking to me is:

One thing I will trust God with today is:

RESPOND

REMEMBER

date:

Today, I feel:

READ

Today, I read:

What stood out to me is:

REFLECT

What I best sense God speaking to me is:

One thing I will trust God with today is:

RESPOND

REMEMBER

date: ....

Today, I feel: ....

READ

Today, I read: ....

What stood out to me is:

REFLECT

What I best sense God speaking to me is:

One thing I will trust God with today is:

RESPOND

REMEMBER

weekly reflection: ....

PERSONAL REFLECTION

What went well this week?

What feeling(s) did I experience most frequently? Why?

Three things I am grateful for are:

1.

2.

3.

RELATIONAL REFLECTION

What went well in my relationships this week?

What felt challenging in my relationships this week?

SPIRITUAL REFLECTION

A theme God has been speaking to me this week through Bible reading, worship, books, or sermons:

Questions I have for God are:

NEXT WEEK

I am looking forward to...

Next week's memory verse:

date: ....

Today, I feel: ....

READ

Today, I read: ....

What stood out to me is:

::

REFLECT

What I best sense God speaking to me is:

::

One thing I will trust God with today is:

::

RESPOND

REMEMBER

date: ....

Today, I feel: ....

READ

Today, I read: ....

What stood out to me is:

REFLECT

What I best sense God speaking to me is:

One thing I will trust God with today is:

RESPOND

REMEMBER

date:

Today, I feel:

READ

Today, I read:

What stood out to me is:

REFLECT

What I best sense God speaking to me is:

One thing I will trust God with today is:

RESPOND

REMEMBER

date:

Today, I feel:

READ

Today, I read:

What stood out to me is:

REFLECT

What I best sense God speaking to me is:

One thing I will trust God with today is:

RESPOND

REMEMBER

date: ....

Today, I feel: ....

READ

Today, I read: ....

What stood out to me is:

REFLECT

What I best sense God speaking to me is:

One thing I will trust God with today is:

RESPOND

REMEMBER

weekly reflection: ....

PERSONAL REFLECTION

What went well this week?

What feeling(s) did I experience most frequently? Why?

Three things I am grateful for are:

1.

2.

3.

RELATIONAL REFLECTION

What went well in my relationships this week?

What felt challenging in my relationships this week?

SPIRITUAL REFLECTION

A theme God has been speaking to me this week through Bible reading, worship, books, or sermons:

Questions I have for God are:

NEXT WEEK

I am looking forward to...

Next week's memory verse:

date: ....

Today, I feel: ....

READ

Today, I read: ....

What stood out to me is:

REFLECT

What I best sense God speaking to me is:

One thing I will trust God with today is:

RESPOND

REMEMBER

date:

Today, I feel:

READ

Today, I read:

What stood out to me is:

REFLECT

What I best sense God speaking to me is:

One thing I will trust God with today is:

RESPOND

REMEMBER

date:

Today, I feel:

READ

Today, I read:

What stood out to me is:

REFLECT

What I best sense God speaking to me is:

One thing I will trust God with today is:

RESPOND

REMEMBER

date:

Today, I feel:

R E A D

Today, I read:

What stood out to me is:

R E F L E C T

What I best sense God speaking to me is:

One thing I will trust God with today is:

RESPOND

REMEMBER

date: ....

Today, I feel: ....

READ

Today, I read: ....

What stood out to me is:

REFLECT

What I best sense God speaking to me is:

One thing I will trust God with today is:

RESPOND

REMEMBER

weekly reflection: ....

PERSONAL REFLECTION

What went well this week?

What feeling(s) did I experience most frequently? Why?

Three things I am grateful for are:

1.

2.

3.

RELATIONAL REFLECTION

What went well in my relationships this week?

What felt challenging in my relationships this week?

SPIRITUAL REFLECTION

A theme God has been speaking to me this week through Bible reading, worship, books, or sermons:

Questions I have for God are:

NEXT WEEK

I am looking forward to...

Next week's memory verse:

resources

memory verses

Psalm 86:15 - But you, Lord, are a compassionate and gracious God, slow to anger and abounding in faithful love and truth.

Psalm 136:1 - Give thanks to the Lord, for he is good. His faithful love endures forever.

Proverbs 17:17 - A friend loves at all times, and a brother is born for a difficult time.

John 3:16 - For God loved the world in this way: He gave his one and only Son, so that everyone who believes in him will not perish but have eternal life.

1 Corinthians 13:13 - Now these three remain: faith, hope, and love—but the greatest of these is love.

1 Corinthians 16:13-14 - Be alert, stand firm in the faith, be courageous, be strong. Do everything in love.

Ephesians 2:4-5 - But God, who is rich in mercy, because of his great love that he had for us, made us alive with Christ even though we were dead in trespasses. You are saved by grace!

Colossians 3:14-15 - Above all, put on love, which is the perfect bond of unity. And let the peace of Christ, to which you were also called in one body, rule your hearts. And be thankful.

1 John 3:16 - This is how we have come to know love: He laid down his life for us. We should also lay down our lives for our brothers and sisters.

1 John 4:10-11 - Love consists in this: not that we loved God, but that he loved us and sent his Son to be the atoning sacrifice for our sins. Dear friends, if God loved us in this way, we also must love one another.

emotions

Try to narrow down your emotions and be specifc about how you are feeling.

Choose the initial emotion you feel (happy, sad, bad, surprised, angry, fearful), then choose an emotion from that column that is most accurate. Remember, be honest with yourself. There are no wrong emotions.

HAPPY

Content
Interested
Proud
Accepted
Powerful
Peaceful
Trusting
Optimistic

BAD

Bored
Busy
Stressed
Tired

SURPRISED

Startled
Confused
Amazed
Excited

ANGRY

Let Down
Humiliated
Bitter
Mad
Aggressive
Frustrated
Distant
Critical

SAD

Lonely
Vulnerable
Despairing
Guilty
Depressed
Hurt

FEARFUL

Scared
Anxious
Insecure
Weak
Rejected
Threatened

reading plan

DAY	VERSES	DAY	VERSES
1	Galatians 1:1-10	18	Ephesians 2:11-22
2	Galatians 1:11-24	19	Ephesians 3:1-13
3	Galatians 2:1-10	20	Ephesians 3:14-21
4	Galatians 2:11-21	21	Ephesians 4:1-16
5	Galatians 3:1-9	22	Ephesians 4:17-32
6	Galatians 3:10-18	23	Ephesians 5:1-7
7	Galatians 3:19-29	24	Ephesians 5:8-20
8	Galatians 4:1-7	25	Ephesians 5:21-33
9	Galatians 4:8-20	26	Ephesians 6:1-9
10	Galatians 4:21-31	27	Ephesians 6:10-24
11	Galatians 5:1-12	28	James 1:1-8
12	Galatians 5:13-26	29	James 1:9-11
13	Galatians 6:1-10	30	James 1:12-18
14	Galatians 6:11-18	31	James 1:19-21
15	Ephesians 1:1-14	32	James 1:22-27
16	Ephesians 1:15-23	33	James 2:1-7
17	Ephesians 2:1-10	34	James 2:8-13

restoring my relationships

When there is conflict in a relationship, we need to learn to recognize our part in the problem and the solution. Restoring a relationship always involves three parts: forgiveness, repentance, and making amends.

Forgiveness

If someone has done something to hurt you, you need to forgive them. The Bible is clear that we are supposed to forgive others even if they don't apologize or make things right.

By forgiving people, we let go of our pain and we release the other person to God. What they did wrong is an issue they need to deal with. Your part is forgiving them.

Repentance

If we have done something wrong in a relationship (and often we can find something we are responsible for, even if the other person hurt us too), we need to ask God's forgiveness. This is called repentance.

Sometimes, even if we have confessed to God and asked his forgiveness, we don't feel forgiven. This isn't because God hasn't forgiven us—he always does! We usually don't feel forgiven if we are still punishing ourselves and feeling ashamed of our actions. This is why we need to forgive ourselves.

If we don't forgive ourselves, we disrespect the grace and mercy that God pours out on us. If God forgives and loves us, it's prideful to think we should punish and hate ourselves.

Making Amends

Making amends means to make things right.

It involves 3 parts:

- Sincere apology
- Change of behavior
- Restitution

APOLOGY

Your apology should be made in person or in writing. It should be specific about what you did that hurt them and the consequences that resulted. This is not a time to discuss what the other person may have done to hurt you—you are taking responsibility for your own actions, not pointing fingers or passing blame. Additionally, it is not your responsibility to encourage their forgiveness, nor is it your right to receive their forgiveness, so do not ask the other person to forgive you.

CHANGE OF BEHAVIOR

An apology without a change in behavior is worthless. Your actions speak louder than your words. True repentance is displayed when we turn away from our sin and act in the opposite way (ie impatient > patient or unloving > loving)

RESTITUTION

Beyond an apology and change of behavior, sometimes there's something we need to fix in order to restore the relationship. This may mean returning what you stole, fixing what you broke, or paying for something to be replaced. This may be easier to see how it applies to tangible objects, but the same applies for people. It's much more difficult to heal a person than to fix a car, but do what you can to make up for the damage you caused to the other person.

prayer of forgiveness

God, I choose to forgive [name]. When he/she [words or situation that caused hurt] it made me feel [emotions and pain].

As I have accepted your forgiveness for my own sins and shortcomings, I offer this forgiveness to [name]. Whether or not he/she deserves my forgiveness and whether he/she asks for forgiveness, I will freely give it because of your death on the cross.

When I see [name] again, help me recall this prayer and let go of any thoughts towards him/her that are not loving and filled with grace. Help me to see him/her the way you do and help me to love him/her as you do.

I pray that [name] would receive your forgiveness and your blessing. Please heal my heart and help me not to allow this hurt to distance myself from others. Thank you for your extravagant love.

Amen.

prayer of repentance

God, forgive me for [words or actions]. My words/actions caused [result of words or actions]. Above all, I know my sin is separating me from you. I am sorry, God.

Help me to see the ways I sin and fall short, and remind me to quickly bring those things to you. Please help me let go of the shame and regret I feel. I know that I don't deserve your extravagant love and endless grace, yet you give them to me freely because you care for me and do not punish me. I forgive myself and let go of all self-hatred.

Thank you for your forgiveness. Help me resist the temptation to repeat my sin or punish myself for my past sins. I accept your forgiveness and move forward in love and grace.

Amen.

prayer for an anxious heart

Jesus, I bring my heart, mind, and soul to you.

As I pause to rest in your presence, I ask you to fill me with more of you.

I release my stress, anxiety, and worry into your
care. Please fill me with your peace.

Help me to fulfill my responsibilities with a joyful spirit,
knowing that every moment of this day is a gift.

Guide me through my day—giving me eyes to see the
people around me the way you see them.

Thank you for your unwavering presence, God.

Amen.

acknowledgments

This journal you hold has the power to transform your relationship with God. That's worth celebrating! So first I want to acknowledge you and the commitment you made to meet regularly with God.

In addition to my gratitude to God for every bit of grace and truth he has spoken into my life, I would like to thank the many others who took part in this work with me.

To the talented team who helped me with all the things that stressed me out: Jennie Scott, Katy Epling, and Sara Ward. Thank you for using your gifts for this project.

A special thank you to my writing mastermind: Cyndee Ownbey, Eva Kubasiak, Jazmin Frank, Katy Epling, Kristin Vanderlip, Sara Ward, and Thelma Nienhuis. Your presence makes this work less lonely and inspires me to keep going.

Thanks also to my extended writing community of hope*writers who supported me through endorsing and sharing this journal. And thank you to my early readers who provided such valuable feedback and helped shape these journals into what they are today.

My beautiful, kind, life-giving kids: Emery, Mia, Tessa, and Lincoln. You teach me every day what it means to love as Jesus does. These journals are for you. May they draw you closer to God and allow the Holy Spirit to comfort, guide, and encourage you no matter what you face in the years to come.

Finally, to my husband, Tynan. For a writer who can string sentences together for a living, words fail me in my deep love for you. I choose you every day.

about the author

Taryn Nergaard is an author and life coach with a passion for helping people find freedom. She is the creator of the *Reflective Bible Journals*, which help kids, teens, and adults hear God's voice and follow his lead. In her years leading a healing-discipleship ministry, she discovered that very few people know what true freedom in Christ feels like. She wants to change that. Taryn believes that surrender is the pathway to freedom, and when we stop holding on to what's holding us back, we experience more hope, joy, peace, and purpose.

Taryn lives in British Columbia, Canada with her husband and four kids. When she's not busy homeschooling or working, you'll find her enjoying a cup of coffee and a good book, or curled up on the couch binge watching her current favorite show.

@tarynnergaard
www.tarynnergaard.com

Made in the USA
Las Vegas, NV
02 December 2021